# WE WERE HERE FIRST
## THE NATIVE AMERICANS

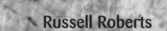

## THE
# CHEROKEE

Russell Roberts

PURPLE TOAD
PUBLISHING

WE WERE HERE FIRST
THE NATIVE AMERICANS

The Apache of the Southwest
The Cherokee
The Cheyenne
The Comanche
The Inuit of the Arctic
The Iroquois of the Northeast
The Lenape
The Navajo
The Nez Perce of the Pacific Northwest
The Sioux of the Great Northern Plains

Copyright © 2016 by Purple Toad Publishing, Inc.

Printing    1    2    3    4    5    6    7    8    9

**PUBLISHER'S NOTE:** The data in this book has been researched in depth, and to the best of our knowledge is factual. Although every measure is taken to give an accurate account, Purple Toad Publishing makes no warranty of the accuracy of the information and is not liable for damages caused by inaccuracies.

Publisher's Cataloging-in-Publication Data
Roberts, Russell.
    Cherokee / written by Russell Roberts.
    p. cm.
Includes bibliographic references and index.
ISBN 9781624691560
1. Cherokee Indians—Juvenile literature. I. Series: We were here first.
E99.C5 2016
 970.5
Library of Congress Control Number:
2015941834

eBook ISBN: 9781624691577

# CONTENTS

The Trail of Tears that the Cherokees and thousands of other Native Americans were forced to take is one of the most shameful episodes in the history of the United States.

# CHAPTER 1
## PEOPLE DIE
## VERY MUCH

August 28, 1838, was a beautiful summer's day at New Echota, Georgia. The sun shone brightly, and puffy white clouds darted across the sky. Sweetly-singing birds flitted from tree to tree in the forest.

Unfortunately for the Cherokee Native Americans who stood alongside a line of wagons winding through the forest, there was little reason to enjoy the fine weather. Most stood there silently, sadness etched on their faces, their hearts heavy with grief. They were about to embark upon *Nunna-da-ul-tsun-yi* (The Place Where They Cried).[1] In American history, it would be known as the Trail of Tears—the forcible removal of the Cherokees from their homeland in the Southeast United States to Oklahoma. The grueling, 800-mile trip had already killed many of their friends and neighbors who had gone before. No one knew if they would be the next to die.

Groups of United States Army soldiers were scattered about on foot and horseback. They would accompany the Cherokees on their trip. The wagons were pulled by either oxen or a combination team of mules and horses. The snorting and nervous pawing of the animals added to the noise and confusion.

As the time to leave approached, Chief Goingsnake mounted his horse and sadly looked around for the last time at the land he loved. Then a shouted command rang through the air: "Move on!"[2] The Cherokees turned west—known to them as the direction of death—and began walking.

Suddenly a low rumble of thunder sounded. Everyone stopped as, in the distance, a dark spiral cloud rose into what had been a sunny and clear sky. It was as if the heavens themselves were screaming in outrage at what was being done to the Cherokees.

Then, as quickly as it had come, the cloud and thunder passed and the sky cleared. A low murmur passed through the assembled Cherokees. Clearly this was a bad omen for their journey to the west.

The Trail of Tears was not just one trip. Because there were so many Cherokees to be moved (more than 15,000), it took numerous times for everyone to reach Oklahoma and other nearby areas. However, no matter

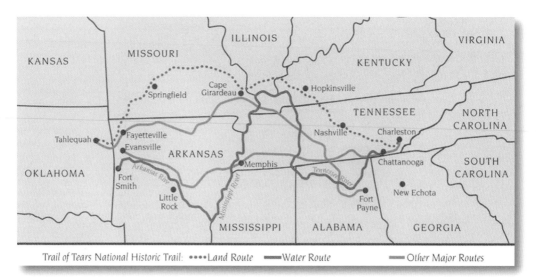

**The Trail of Tears uprooted the Cherokees and other native peoples from their ancestral homes in the southeastern U.S. and forced them to journey to a new home hundreds of miles away.**

when they went, the journey was every bit as horrible as the Native Americans had feared.

The sun beat down on them mercilessly. When no rain came and the earth dried up, the huge group kicked up giant, choking dust clouds. Rain turned the roads to mud, which splattered over everything and everyone. At night, the temperature dropped and the cold often caused teeth to chatter and tongues to stutter. Sometimes the ground was so hard and cold that it hurt the Cherokees' feet as they walked.

With barely enough room in the wagons for the sick and weary, most of the men, women, children, and the elderly walked.

"Multitudes [went] on foot," said one observer, "even aged females, apparently ready to drop into the grave, were traveling with heavy burdens attached to the back—on the sometimes frozen ground, and sometimes muddy streets, with no covering for the feet except what nature had given them."[3]

Wagons broke down and had to be repaired. What little clothing the Cherokees had fell apart and could not be repaired. The food provided—salt pork and dried corn—was scarce and did not provide the nutrition the Cherokees needed. Sometimes turkey

**Many Cherokees did not survive the Trail of Tears. Elizabeth Brown was one of those who did.**

Today, the remaining parts of the Trail of Tears appear peaceful. However, the journey the Cherokees took along it was one of incredible hardship.

and deer could be hunted to supplement this meager diet—sometimes not. When it did not rain, water holes dried up, and those that remained were likely contaminated by disease.

Fatigue, exhaustion, malnutrition, and exposure to the elements caused many of the Cherokee to become ill with measles, whooping cough, dysentery (an intestinal disease that causes fever, diarrhea, and other symptoms), and respiratory infections. Many Cherokees died every day, and were buried in hastily dug graves.

"At one time," said a soldier, "I saw stretched around me and in a few feet of each other, eight of these afflicted creatures [Cherokees] dead or dying."[4]

"Long time we travel on way to new land," remembered one Cherokee. "Women cry . . . children cry . . . many men cry. Many days pass and people die very much."[5]

The wagon drivers were told to keep moving. When a native got toosick to walk, he or she was tossed into a wagon—something everyone tried desperately to avoid. The ill would stumble along in the arms of family and friends, barely able to put one foot in front of the other but afraid of being put into a wagon and separated from loved ones.

Approximately 4,000 Cherokees died on the Trail of Tears, or nearly one-quarter of the people who were forced to take the journey.[6]

How had it come to this? How did a people who were trying to become more like the Americans so that they could live in peace with

Even death did not interrupt the Trail of Tears. Those who died along the way were quickly buried so as not to slow the trip down.

ETERNAL FLAME OF THE
CHEROKEE NATION
THIS FIRE IS A MEMORIAL TO THOSE
PEOPLE WHO SUFFERED AND DIED ON
THE INFAMOUS "TRAIL OF TEARS."
IT ALSO COMMEMORATES THE REUNITING
OF THE EASTERN AND WESTERN
CHEROKEE NATIONS HERE AT RED CLAY
AUG. 7, 1837 — APR. 6, 1984

**Memorials to the incredible pain and suffering of the Cherokees line the Trail of Tears. This eternal flame in Red Clay State Park in Tennessee is one of them.**

them wind up on the Trail of Tears? Why were a people who trusted the United States and its government treated so poorly?

The answers to those questions illuminate one of the darkest periods in the history of the United States.

# A Cherokee Creation Story: How the World Was Made

**As with many other cultures, the Cherokees explained the beginning of the world with a creation story.**

In the beginning, the entire earth consisted of water. All the animals lived on a platform floating in the sky. The platform got too crowded, so the animals sent the Water Beetle down to explore the earth. The Water Beetle dove into the water and swam down until he reached the bottom, which was made of soft mud. The Water Beetle brought the soft mud to the surface. It hardened and formed the earth's crust.

The animals sent the Buzzard down to explore this new ground. As the Buzzard flew, his wings sometimes dipped so low that they made holes in the ground. These became valleys. When the Buzzard's wings rose up, mountains were created.

Once on earth, the animals and plants were told by the gods to stay awake for seven nights. However, only the Owl, Panther, and a few other animals did. They were granted the ability to see at night. Of the plants, only the holly, cedar, pine, and spruce trees stayed awake. They were rewarded by being allowed to keep their foliage all year long, while the others lost theirs as winter approached.

The Cherokees first encountered Europeans when Spanish explorer Hernando De Soto came upon them while he was searching for gold.

# CHAPTER 2
## THE EUROPEANS COME

The Cherokees once lived in the Great Lakes region. However, conflict with other tribes in the area caused them to move to what would someday become the Southeast United States. There they settled into territory that would eventually become parts of many states: Alabama, Georgia, Kentucky, North Carolina, South Carolina, Tennessee, Virginia, and West Virginia.

The Cherokees spoke a language similar to that of the Iroquois, who lived farther north. They were the southernmost tribe to speak this tongue. Their name for themselves was *Ani-yun-wiya,* which in the Iroquois language meant "real people."[1] One theory is that the name *Cherokee* came from the Creeks, a neighboring tribe, who called them *tciloki,* which means "people of the different speech."[2] Another possible origin of the word *Cherokee* is from the Choctaw tribe's word *Chillaki,* which means "cave dweller."[3]

The Cherokees first encountered Europeans in May 1540. Spanish conquistador Hernando De Soto was searching for gold, and came to the area from the Gulf Coast with a group of soldiers. The natives greeted him with baskets of berries, but De Soto did not stay. Thereafter, the Spaniards often came into contact with the Cherokees.

When English settlers started building villages in the southeast, such as Jamestown, Virginia, they encountered the Cherokees, who were living in the same area.

Although the Cherokees sometimes saw French traders, the Europeans who made the biggest impact on them were the English. Once the English built settlements along the Atlantic coast, such as Jamestown (Virginia) in 1607, contact between them and the Cherokees increased. Unlike the Spanish, who were mainly interested in gold, the English wanted land. They built towns, chopped down trees to clear areas for farming, and steadily pushed westward into the forest.

"I have discovered a Country so dilitious [possibly "delicious"], pleasant and fruitful that were it cultivated doubtless it would prove a Second Paradise," wrote one explorer of Cherokee lands in Kentucky.[4]

By the end of the 17th century, many Cherokee villages had English traders living in them. The traders brought items such as brass kettles, metal

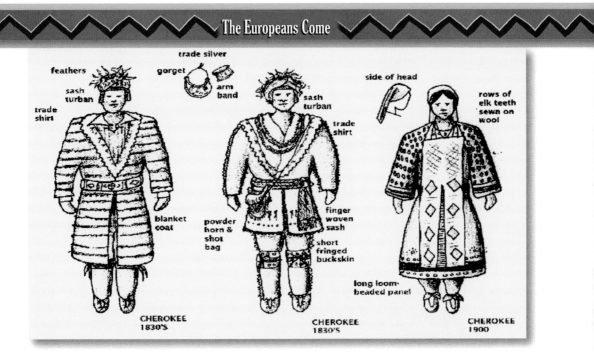

Cherokee women wore clothing made of deerskin, since deer were so abundant in the forests near their homes. Deerskins were also highly sought after by people in Europe.

hatchets, and scissors. They also provided the Cherokees with guns and ammunition.

The main item the traders obtained from the Cherokees in return was deerskins, which were in great demand in Europe. From deerskins the Europeans made gloves, knee breeches, and other leather items. The abundance of deerskins among the Cherokees gave the English the mistaken impression that they were hunters and gatherers, or those who obtain all of their food from wild plants and animals rather than by farming. The reality was that Cherokee society was primarily based on agriculture.

To the English, hunting and gathering was a simple form of society. Thus, they considered the Cherokees uncivilized, and their use of the land inadequate. The English believed they were making better use of the land they took away from the Cherokees and other tribes.

It was even thought that native land was so fertile that crops sprang up entirely on their own, with no help from the natives people Even an intelligent man like Thomas Jefferson wrote, ". . . all the nations of Indians in North America lived in the hunter state and depended for subsistence [things they needed to survive] on hunting, fishing, and the spontaneous fruits of the earth."[5]

In 1721, a treaty negotiated between the Cherokees and Governor Francis Nicholson of Charlestown (South Carolina) regulated trading methods and established boundary lines between Cherokee land and English land. This was the first time that the Cherokees gave away land to the English. They hoped that by doing so, it would establish a boundary between the two.

A census in that year reported that the Cherokees lived in 53 towns and numbered 10,379 individuals; 3,510 of these were warriors. By 1735, these numbers had increased to 64 towns containing about 17,000 people, with more than 6,000 as warriors.[6]

In 1738, a smallpox epidemic broke out among the native tribes in the area, including the Cherokees. Smallpox had been brought by the Europeans, and since the natives had never been exposed to it, they had no immunity or treatment against it. The disease swept through them like wildfire. One estimate is that almost half of the Cherokees perished from smallpox.

As one observer said, the Cherokees "died like rotten sheep."[7]

Those who caught smallpox and survived were horrified by the way the disease left scars all over their faces.

but even greater disasters lay ahead for the Cherokees.

**Europeans brought diseases like smallpox to the New World. The illnesses swept through the Cherokee and other Native American tribes.**

# The Cherokees in London

When Cherokee chiefs traveled to London, England, in 1730, Londoners constantly stared at them, because they had never seen Native American people before.

As the French advanced farther into North America, the English worried that they would one day take it over, so they searched for allies against them. A logical place to find them was the Native American tribes who already lived there, such as the Cherokees.

In 1730, seven Cherokee representatives were brought to London by Sir Alexander Cuming. There, they were the talk of the town, with crowds following them around and innkeepers charging to let people peer at them in their rooms. European-style clothes were made for each, which the natives wore while they had their portraits painted. The Real People also had an audience with King George II.

The result of this visit to London was that the Cherokees agreed to trade only with the English, to forbid any other whites from entering their country, and to return any white lawbreakers they found on their lands. In exchange, the English offered friendship and protection "for as long as the mountains and rivers last, and the sun shines."[8]

Cherokee dwellings were very similar to the cabins in which European settlers lived.

# CHAPTER 3
## CHEROKEE LIFE

The Cherokees were known as one of the Five Civilized Tribes. The others were their neighbors in the Southeast: the Creeks, Choctaws, Chickasaws, and Seminoles.

Cherokee villages were usually located alongside rivers and streams, so that they could farm the rich soil found there. The Real People grew a variety of crops, including beans, squash, pumpkins, tobacco, and sunflowers. They also grew three different types of corn: one for roasting, another for boiling, and a third type for grinding into flour to make cornbread.

Women performed most of the daily farming activities. Men assisted by clearing land and planting, and when harvest time arrived both sexes worked to bring in the crops. Cherokee families were oriented toward the mother, rather than the father. They lived in the mother's household, and farm fields were passed along from mother to daughter.

Unlike Europeans, with traditions of private property, Cherokees owned their land in common—meaning that the land belonged to all. Anyone had the right to clear and use land as long as it did not affect their neighbors. The fields were divided into separate sections, but everyone worked together doing chores such as hoeing and planting, moving from one

Cherokee families grew gardens near their homes. These smaller crops added to those grown in the fields, which fed the whole village.

family's land to another's. Each family also had a small garden near their home.

The Cherokees were skillful hunters. Large game, such as bear, deer, and buffalo, were rapidly disappearing in the Southeast as more and more land was developed. Still, the Cherokees hunted them when they could, either with guns or bows and arrows. The hunters each wore a deerskin complete with antlers so that they looked like deer and could sneak up close to their targets.

Smaller game was hunted with blowguns made from the hollowed-out stems of a cane plant. The darts that the hunters blew through these blowguns were accurate up to 60 feet.[1]

The Cherokees fished with hooks and lines. They also used a substance made from Yucca *filamentosa* plants to stun fish and bring them to the

surface, where they could easily collect them.

The Yucca plant provided a substance that the Cherokees used for fishing.

Even though they used the land and its animals, the Cherokees had great respect for all living creatures. When any animal (except bears) was killed, songs, prayers, and ceremonies were performed. By using almost the entire animal—hides were tanned, meat eaten, bones and antlers turned into tools, sinew made into thread—the Real People showed their respect for the creature.

This respect extended to other gifts that Nature provided. The Cherokees made dugout canoes from large trees, wove baskets and mats from river cane plants, and turned river clay into pots.

Hollowing out trees to make dugout canoes is just one of many ways that the Cherokees used their natural resources.

The Cherokees felt a special relationship with the land and wanted to make certain that their children's children could benefit from it as much as they did.

"The land was given to us by the Great Spirit above as our common right," said a group of Cherokee women in 1818, "to raise our children upon and to make support for our rising generations."[2]

Cherokee families often had two houses—one for summer and one for winter. Summer houses were larger, rectangular, and had peaked roofs made of bark or thatch. The walls consisted of a combination of cane and clay. Winter homes had cone-shaped roofs. They were built over fire pits so they could double as sweathouses.

The main building in a Cherokee town was the council house. This seven-sided structure had a bark roof and was constructed of tall log pillars and wooden crossbeams. It could hold up to 500 people. Townspeople would gather there and listen to important issues being discussed, such as how to make up for a bad harvest. Individual homes surrounded the public areas of town.

The Cherokees had seven clans, or families, that could supposedly trace their origins back to a single ancestor. These clan members were located throughout the villages. The clans provided protection for their members. If someone had something wrong done to them, the clan would try to fix the situation.

The Cherokees lived a life ruled by the seasons, and marked the passage of time by celebrating several festivals throughout the year. One of the most important was the Green Corn Festival, which other tribes, such as the Creeks, also celebrated.

The Green Corn Festival took place at the end of the summer, when the last corn crop ripened. It lasted between four and eight days. In preparation for the festival, men repaired the communal buildings (such as the council house) while women cleaned their homes and cooking utensils and put out their hearth fires. Chiefs, shamans, warriors, and village elders fasted and lit the Sacred Fire. Then they had a feast where they ate corn and drank the

Like other Native American tribes, the Cherokees enjoyed sports and contests, such as lacrosse and racing.

Black Drink, which caused them to vomit and was supposed to purify the body.

At this point, the remaining villagers joined in the celebration. They took coals from the Sacred Fire and relit their individual home fires. Then they prepared a large deer meat feast for all. Dancing and contests in such sports as archery and lacrosse were held. The ceremony ended with everyone taking a purification bath in the river. By doing so the Cherokees wiped out the stains of the old year, and prepared for the new one clear in mind and body. To emphasize that this was indeed a new beginning, all the wrongs of the past year—except murder—were forgiven.

Cherokee towns were divided into two groups called the Red and the White. The White Group controlled things during times of peace. The White Chief (also known as the Most Beloved Man) was in charge of council meetings and gave advice on everything from farming to lawmaking to disputes between individuals.

In times of war or when the village was threatened, the Red Group took control. The Red war chief was a veteran warrior who had made his reputation in battle. A war council gave him advice. One important job of the war chief was to select the War Woman. She accompanied the war parties, but did not take part in the actual battles. The War Woman helped feed the warriors, gave advice, and decided which prisoners would live and which would die.

When a Cherokee town changed from peace to war, the warriors fasted and danced so that they would become warlike. This change from peacemaker to warrior was presided over by the *Adawehi,* who wore shell necklaces that contained river pearls. This showed that the *Adawehi* knew the secrets of the stars. After the war period was over, the warriors went through a purifying ritual to prepare for peaceful life once more.

The Cherokees' view of Europeans was not positive. "They frequently tell us," said English trader John Adair in 1738, "that though we are possessed of a great deal of yellow and white stone [gold and silver] . . . and everything else our hearts delight in . . . these things seem to create in us much toil and pain instead of ease and pleasure . . . and therefore they say we are truly poor, and deserve pity instead of envy."[3]

The Cherokees' opinion of the settlers would continue to decline as the Europeans thirsted for new land.

**The Cherokees were known as fierce fighters.**

# The War Between People and Animals

Another Cherokee story explains their hunting trials.

Long ago, plants, animals, and people lived together in peace and harmony. However, the number of people increased so fast that they started crowding the bigger animals. Even worse, people invented weapons that they used to kill the animals.

The animals decided to make war upon humans. However, when bears tried to use bows and arrows, their claws were too big for the bowstrings. Thus, bears never got revenge for all their members who had been killed.

Deer, however, used their spiritual power to send rheumatism (a condition that makes joints ache, particularly in wet weather) to hurt people. When other animals saw that this was successful they too sent diseases to affect humans. The animals wished to punish those who did not show the proper respect toward the animals they killed.

When the plants saw what was happening, they decided to help people by providing cures for the diseases all the animals (except the bears) had sent. The Cherokees began performing rituals to show respect for the animals they killed, so they could avoid illnesses. However, since bears had sent no illnesses, the rituals did not include them.

When the French and Indian War began in 1754, the Cherokees sided with the English.

# CHAPTER 4
# CHANGING
# TIMES

The Cherokees were just recovering from the devastation of the smallpox epidemic when the French and Indian War began in North America in 1754. Like other Native American nations, the Real People were caught in the middle of the conflict between the French and English. They were forced to choose sides. The Cherokees sided with the English, because their trade with them had become important. The English appreciated the Cherokees' fighting skills. A young Virginia soldier named George Washington wrote: "They are more serviceable than twice their number of white men . . . If they return to their nation, no words can tell how much they will be missed."[1]

The English repeatedly made treaties with the Cherokees to try to keep them loyal. Unfortunately, these treaties almost always contained language that deprived the Cherokees of land. (One estimate is that between 1721 and 1777, the Cherokees gave up half their land in treaties with the English.)[2]

Relations between the two sides began deteriorating in 1758. A group of 100 Cherokees was returning home through Virginia territory after assisting in a campaign to take Fort Duquesne (modern-day Pittsburgh) from the French. They

The Cherokees assisted in the battle to take France's Fort Duquesne (pronounced doo-KAYN), but a misunderstanding after the fight ruined relations between the two sides.

came upon some horses running loose. Since some of the Cherokees had lost their horses while helping the English, they thought it was proper to replace them with these. English settlers disagreed. They attacked the Cherokees, killing between twelve and forty of them, scalping them, and turning in the scalps for money.

The two sides began skirmishing with each other. Cherokee chiefs thought they had arranged for peace in May 1759, but South Carolina Governor Henry Lyttelton suddenly demanded that every Cherokee who had killed a white settler be handed over for execution. The Cherokees refused, and Lyttelton declared war on them in November of that year.

For the next year, the flames of war burned throughout the frontier as both sides committed atrocities against one another. In 1761, an uneasy peace took hold when the Cherokees signed a peace treaty with Virginia. The following year they did the same with South Carolina.

Realizing that friction with Native Americans was growing, in 1763 England's King George III issued a Royal Proclamation that forbade English settlement west of the Appalachian Mountains. Some of this land was Cherokee territory. Ironically, this meant that individual people could not buy native land. Only governments could buy land, if they negotiated with the

**King George III**

natives. This restriction bothered many people who wanted to move farther west but were forbidden to. It was one of the decisions that turned many colonists against England and led to the American Revolution.

The 1763 proclamation was one reason that some Cherokees fought with the English against the colonists during the American Revolution. The natives were realizing that the American colonists were the real threat to them, not the English, for many colonists had ignored the king's proclamation and settled on Cherokee lands. A Cherokee leader named Old Tassel summed up the natives' situation: "We are a poor distressed people that is in great trouble. We have no place to hunt on. [Do not] take our lands from us that the Great Man above gave us. It is ours."[3]

The war took a severe toll on the Cherokees. Virginia and South Carolina raised soldiers specifically to fight the Real People. More than 50 of their towns were destroyed, livestock and fields were ruined, and many people were killed.[4] In 1785, after the war ended, the Cherokees signed the Treaty of Hopewell with the new United States government. In exchange for giving up yet more land, the treaty promised that there would be no further white intrusion on the remaining Cherokee lands.

**War chief Dragging Canoe tried to stop the Europeans from settling on Cherokee land by chasing away surveyors and smashing their equipment.**

Unfortunately, there were already over 3,000 people living illegally on Cherokee land, and the treaty did not require them to leave.[5] A war chief named Dragging Canoe took matters into his own hands, leading his warriors in attacks on the settler cabins that were popping up all over Cherokee land. Whenever the warriors discovered surveyors marking their land, meaning that whites were about to settle on it, they chased them away and smashed their compasses, which they called Land Stealers.

The fighting alarmed George Washington, the first president of the United States. Washington wanted to stop treating Native Americans like enemies who had no rights to land. Secretary of War Henry Knox summed up the official view: "The Indians being the prior occupants, possess the right to soil. To dispossess them . . . would be a gross violation of the fundamental laws of nature . . . ."[6]

Thus, in 1791, the United States and the Cherokees signed the Treaty of Holston. The treaty prohibited natives from trading or having diplomatic relations with any other country. In exchange, the Cherokees were promised once again that no more whites would be allowed to settle on their land. They would also receive a yearly payment of $1,000 for the lands already lost.

However, the most significant part of the treaty said that the Cherokees were to become "civilized." This meant the government expected them to give up hunting and fur trading and become full-time farmers. The Cherokees agreed to this because they had little choice. They had tried fighting, and they had tried signing away land, and neither had stopped the whites from advancing farther into Cherokee territory. Something else had to be done, or the Real People would become extinct.

After this, it became the official policy of the U.S. government to "civilize" Cherokees. All natives were to raise crops on their small piece of land, and to embrace Christianity. Since the natives would no longer need vast

**This monument in Knoxville, Tennessee, commemorates the signing of the Treaty of Holston between the United States and the Cherokee.**

amounts of land for hunting, the whites could obtain it for their towns and farms.

In 1792, Dragging Canoe died and was given an honored burial. Twenty years earlier he had predicted that the whites would someday drive the Real People off their ancestral lands to a distant place. Little did the remaining Cherokees realize how soon Dragging Canoe's words would come true.

**Dragging Canoe**

# Major Ridge

Major Ridge was a full-blood Cherokee and one of the tribe's most respected leaders who supported "civilization" efforts.

Born in 1771 in modern-day Tennessee, Ridge in his youth was a strong warrior and was initially called Nunnehidihi (He Who Slays the Enemy In His Path). Later, he was called Ganundalegi (The Man Who Walks On the Mountain Top). Another translation of "Mountain Top" is Ridge. After fighting alongside Andrew Jackson in the 1814 Creek War, he was given the first name Major.

At 21, Ridge became a member of the Cherokee Council, a prestigious position. He realized that the "civilization" program was the best way for the Cherokees to save themselves. He reportedly told Tecumseh when he came to recruit warriors to fight the whites that he would kill him if he spread his anti-civilization message among his people.

Wholeheartedly embracing "civilization," Ridge became a wealthy plantation owner, even owning over two dozen slaves. In December 1835, he signed the Treaty of New Echota, which required the Cherokees to move west and resulted in the Trail of Tears. As he signed, Ridge said, "I have signed my death warrant."[7]

One year after the Cherokees' march, Ridge was assassinated.

**Major Ridge**

Sequoyah developed the Cherokee alphabet.

# CHAPTER 5
## THE ROAD TO THE TRAIL OF TEARS

While some Cherokees resisted "civilization," others accepted it as their only hope of survival. By 1819, some had adopted white ways so successfully that John C. Calhoun, Secretary of War, told the Cherokees, "[You are] now becoming like the white people."[1]

Many of the Cherokees had realized that if they did not become more like white people, they would perish. A Cherokee named George Guess, also called Sequoyah, developed an alphabet of Cherokee sounds and marks so that the natives could communicate like the whites. They established a newspaper called the *Cherokee Phoenix* in 1828. They formed a government that, in 1827, held a constitutional convention—just like the whites had done. They even wrote a Cherokee constitution that promised ". . . to establish justice, promote our common welfare, and secure to ourselves and our posterity the blessings of liberty."[2] These words were a direct echo of the U.S. Constitution.

Unfortunately, the Cherokees also followed the American way of African-American slavery. For the Cherokees, slaves were not considered family, they were not taken as wives or husbands, and they were not educated. They were also denied citizenship rights.[3] (African-American slaves accompanied the Cherokees on the Trail of Tears. They suffered hardships as greatly as did the natives.)

As the federal government attempted to "civilize" the natives, another idea of dealing with the Southeastern tribes arose: moving them from the southeast to the west.

For years the idea had been circulating in Washington, D.C., that the Cherokees really wanted to move out West, but were prevented from doing so by tribe members who stubbornly clung to the old ways, or by Cherokees like Major Ridge who had grown prosperous and were unwilling to give up everything and move. President Thomas Jefferson had first proposed the western move in 1803, and since then several thousand Cherokees, Creeks, and others had moved there voluntarily.

Soon, however, state populations exploded. In 1810, the combined population of Ohio, Tennessee, and Georgia was 40,000; in 1830 it was 445,000.[4] More land was needed to accommodate all those new people. The native tribes held that land, and the whites wanted it.

By 1826, the Georgia legislature had already forced most of the Creek Nation to leave their ancestral lands and move west. Now they concentrated on the Cherokees, who possessed five million acres in northwestern Georgia.[5] In 1828, after calling on the federal government to remove the Real People and condemning their constitution as outrageous, Georgia passed a law stating that if the Cherokees did not move west by January 1830, the state would extend its authority over all Cherokee land and declare all laws and actions of the Cherokee government null and void. In effect, the state could do whatever it wanted to the Cherokees.

A second blow struck the Cherokees in 1828 when Andrew Jackson was elected the seventh president of the United States. The Real People were aware of Jackson's views. (Jackson had previously said that he felt the Cherokees were "ripe for emigration [to the West]"[6]) Even though he had once fought beside them against the Creeks in 1814, and he knew their culture well, he wanted them to move.

Chief Junaluska, who had fought alongside Jackson in the Battle of Horseshoe Bend during the Creek War, said: "If I had known that Jackson

**Andrew Jackson was a veteran Indian fighter who had seized millions of acres of Native American land as part of the settlement that ended the Creek War.**

would drive us from our homes, I would have killed him that day on the Horseshoe."[7]

In his inaugural address on March 4, 1829, Jackson made his intentions clear: he planned to move all southeastern tribes west. This, he added, would be best for the tribes, for it would free them from white men always bothering them. He submitted a bill to Congress authorizing removal.

Despite the Cherokees' efforts to become "civilized" in the eyes of the federal government, Congress passed the bill. Jackson signed it on May 28, 1830.

Now that it was inevitable that the Cherokees were going to lose their land, people began looking forward to the imminent availability of new land. They sang: *"All I ask in this creation, Is a pretty little wife and a big plantation, Way up yonder in the Cherokee Nation."*[8]

The Cherokees did not go quietly. Some of their most respected leaders, including Major Ridge and Elias Boudinot (publisher

**Andrew Jackson**

**Elias Boudinot**

of the *Cherokee Phoenix*) toured the country denouncing the decision. Soon, the question of Cherokee removal was being debated all over the United States.

Ultimately, some Northern lawyers volunteered to argue the Cherokees' case before the U.S. Supreme Court. On March 4, 1832, the court, under Chief Justice John Marshall, heard arguments in the case of *Samuel A. Worcester v. The State of Georgia.* Shortly thereafter, the court issued its ruling in favor of the Cherokees. "The Cherokee Nation is a distinct community," the Court said in its decision, "occupying its own territory . . . in which the laws of Georgia can have no right to enter but with the consent of the Cherokees."[9]

**Chief Justice John Marshall**

The Cherokees celebrated the decision. Boudinot wrote, "The question is forever settled as to who is right and who is wrong."[10]

It soon became clear that it didn't matter who was right and who was wrong. The Cherokees were still going to be forced to move, because Jackson had no intention of obeying the court. "John Marshall has made his decision," he snapped. "Now let him enforce it."[11]

Georgia also ignored the U.S. Supreme Court. Before long, hundreds of surveyors were tramping all over Cherokee land, dividing up into segments, preparing for a state-sponsored land lottery of Cherokee territory.

**John Ross**

The realization that the Supreme Court decision meant nothing made influential Cherokees, such as Major Ridge, his son, John, and Elias Boudinot, decide that the best hope for their people lay in negotiating a good deal for them out west. Chief John Ross continued to fight against the removal.

On December 29, 1835, the Ridges and Elias Boudinot signed the Treaty of New Echota. In return for relocating west, the Cherokees would receive $5 million and a large land parcel.

Ross produced a petition with 15,000 signatures that claimed the treaty was invalid because it did not reflect the will of the majority of the Cherokee people. Ignoring the petition, the U.S. Senate approved the treaty in May 1836. The treaty set the date for removal as May 23, 1838.

This is how the Cherokees found themselves on the Trail of Tears.

Retribution for signing the Treaty of New Echota was swift. Cherokee blood law dictated death for anyone who sold any more lands. On June 22, 1839, the Ridges and Boudinot were assassinated by other Cherokees.

The first years for the Cherokees in the west were difficult. Rivers flooded, washing away their crops. The soil was hard to plow, often requiring two horses when a family was lucky to have one. Planting crops shallower just dried them out.

Somehow, the Cherokees survived. Ripped away from their homeland and sent 800 miles away, the Cherokees not only survived, but prospered.

Today the Cherokee nation, with over 317,000 citizens, is the largest tribal nation in the United States. The largest Cherokee Indian population lives in Oklahoma, which contains three federally-recognized Cherokee communities. They are an important part of the area's economy, with an annual impact of more than $1.5 billion. They are a vital people with a

**Drummers at the Cherokee Celebration in Tulsa, Oklahoma**

vibrant culture and heritage. They celebrate their rich ancestral history while looking optimistically to the future.

"We are not a people of the past," said Principal Chief Chad Smith in 2005. "We are a people of the present, and for many centuries, we will be a people of the future."[12]

The Seal of the Cherokee Nation commemorates the signing of the Cherokee Nation Constitution that was adopted after the Trail of Tears.

# Sequoyah

| | a | | | | e | | i | | | o | | u | | v [ə] | |
|---|---|---|---|---|---|---|---|---|---|---|---|---|---|---|---|
| D | a | | | R | e | | T | i | | Ꭳ | o | Ꮕ | u | i | v |
| Ꮡ | ga | Ꭴ | ka | Ꮎ | ge | | Ꮹ | gi | | A | go | J | gu | E | gv |
| Ꮀ | ha | | | Ꮄ | he | | ᏹ | hi | | Ꮵ | ho | Ꮧ | hu | Ꮕ | hv |
| W | la | | | Ꮧ | le | | Ꮮ | li | | Ꮐ | lo | M | lu | Ꮧ | lv |
| Ꮉ | ma | | | Ꮞ | me | | H | mi | | Ꮝ | mo | Ꮀ | mu | | |
| Ꮎ | na | Ꮏ | hna | Ꮐ | nah | Ꮅ | ne | Ꮒ | ni | Z | no | Ꮗ | nu | Ꮕ | nv |
| Ꮖ | qua | | | Ꮗ | que | | Ꮞ | qui | | Ꮘ | quo | Ꮜ | quu | Ꮾ | quv |
| Ꮪ | s | Ꮜ | sa | Ꮞ | se | | Ꮟ | si | | Ꮢ | so | Ꮯ | su | R | sv |
| Ꮣ | da | Ꮤ | ta | Ꮥ | de | Ꮦ | te | Ꮧ | di | Ꮨ | ti | V | do | Ꮪ | du | Ꮫ | dv |
| Ꮬ | dla | Ꮭ | tla | Ꮮ | tle | | Ꮯ | tli | | Ꮰ | tlo | Ꮱ | tlu | Ꮲ | tlv |
| Ꮳ | tsa | | | Ꮴ | tse | | Ꮵ | tsi | | K | tso | Ꮷ | tsu | Ꮶ | tsv |
| Ꮹ | wa | | | Ꮺ | we | | Ꮻ | wi | | Ꮼ | wo | Ꮽ | wu | Ꮾ | wv |
| Ꮿ | ya | | | Ᏸ | ye | | Ᏹ | yi | | Ᏺ | yo | Ᏻ | yu | B | yv |

**Sequoyah's Alphabet**

Sequoyah, also known as George Guess, developed the Cherokee alphabet. He was born in 1770 in Tennessee. His mother was a member of one of the seven original Cherokee clans.

Sequoyah was a silversmith engraver, and this got him interested in the written language of the whites. In 1809, he began to develop a Cherokee alphabet by writing down signs connected to individual sounds. Soon, he had developed a syllabary (a set of written symbols) composed of individual Cherokee characters for each distinct sound that could be combined into written words. (There were 85 total.) Sequoyah used pokeberry juice to write down the signs and sounds on bark.

His six-year-old daughter quickly learned his alphabet. To demonstrate its effectiveness, Sequoyah would send his daughter away, then write down a message. When his daughter returned, she would see the marks he had made and speak the sentence.

The Cherokees began learning this alphabet. When Elias Boudinot's *Cherokee Phoenix* began in 1827, it printed in both Cherokee and English. Sequoyah eventually left the Southeast to live along the Arkansas River. He died in 1843.

1. The Cherokees were raising corn as early as 1,000 BC.

2. After Sequoyah showed his alphabet system to the Cherokee people, more than 80% of them learned it in just a few months.

3. Typically, between 30–50 families would live in a single Cherokee village.

4. The Cherokee played a game similar to lacrosse that was called Anejodi.

5. To escape relocation, some Cherokee hid in the Allegheny Mountains.

6. On June 23, 1865, Stand Watie was the last Confederate general to lay down his arms after the Union and Confederates agreed to a peace treaty.

7. Corn, beans, and squash were known to the Cherokee as "The Three Sisters."

8. The water drum, a traditional Cherokee musical instrument, was a pot or kettle with an inch of water or other liquid inside and a skin stretched over top.

9. The Cherokee flag contains a black star in memory of those who died on the Trail of Tears.

10. The Cherokee traditionally had seven directions: north, south, east, west, up, down, and center (where you are).

### Chapter One

1. Peter Collier, *When Shall They Rest? The Cherokees' Long Struggle with America.* (New York: Holt, Rinehart, and Winston, 1973), p. 76.
2. Daniel Blake Smith, *An American Betrayal: Cherokee Patriots and the Trail of Tears.* (New York: Henry Holt and Company, 2011), p. 216.
3. Ibid, p. 231.
4. Theda Perdue and Michael D. Green, *The Cherokee Nation and the Trail of Tears.* (New York, The Penguin Group, 2007), p. 121.
5. John Ehle, *Trail of Tears: The Rise and Fall of the Cherokee Nation.* (New York: Anchor Books, 1988), p. 358.
6. Perdue and Green, p. 139.

### Chapter Two

1. Carl Waldman, *Encyclopedia of Native American Tribes.* (New York: Facts on File Publications, 1988), p. 43.
2. Ibid.
3. Peter Collier, *When Shall They Rest? The Cherokees' Long Struggle with America.* (New York: Holt, Rinehart, and Winston, 1973), p. 9.
4. Ibid. p. 12.
5. Theda Perdue and Michael D. Green, *The Cherokee Nation and the Trail of Tears.* (New York: The Penguin Group, 2007), p. 13.
6. James Mooney, *Myths of the Cherokee.* (New York: Dover Publications, Inc., 1995), p. 34.
7. Collier, p. 7.
8. Ibid., p. 19.

### Chapter Three

1. Carl Waldman, *Encyclopedia of Native American Tribes.* (New York: Facts on File Publications, 1988), p. 44.
2. Theda Perdue and Michael D. Green, *The Cherokee Nation and the Trail of Tears.* (New York: The Penguin Group, 2007), p. 6.

3. Peter Collier, *When Shall They Rest? The Cherokees' Long Struggle with America.* (New York: Holt, Rinehart, and Winston, 1973), p. 17.

### Chapter Four

1. Peter Collier, *When Shall They Rest? The Cherokees' Long Struggle with America.* (New York: Holt, Rinehart, and Winston, 1973), p. 21.
2. Theda Perdue and Michael D. Green, *The Cherokee Nation and the Trail of Tears.* (New York: The Penguin Group, 2007), p. 17.
3. Collier, p. 23.
4. Daniel Blake Smith, *An American Betrayal: Cherokee Patriots and the Trail of Tears.* (New York: Henry Holt and Company, 2011), p. 11.
5. Collier, p. 25.
6. Smith, p. 11.
7. Ibid. p. 176.

### Chapter Five

1. Daniel Blake Smith, *An American Betrayal: Cherokee Patriots and the Trail of Tears.* (New York: Henry Holt and Company, 2011), p. 29.
2. Theda Perdue and Michael D. Green, *The Cherokee Nation and the Trail of Tears.* (New York: The Penguin Group, 2007), p. 40.
3. John Ehle, *Trail of Tears: The Rise and Fall of the Cherokee Nation.* (New York: Anchor Books, 1988), p. 142.
4. Perdue and Green, p. 49.
5. Ibid, p. 57.
6. Smith, p. 92.
7. Peter Collier, *When Shall They Rest? The Cherokees' Long Struggle with America.* (New York: Holt, Rinehart, and Winston, 1973), p. 53.
8. Smith, p. 96.
9. Collier, p. 63.
10. Ibid. p. 63.
11. Smith, p. 136.
12. Perdue and Green, p. 164.

### Books

Allen, Nancy Kelly. *First Fire: A Cherokee Folktale.* Mount Pleasant, SC: Sylvan Dell Publishing, 2014.

Bruchac, Joseph. *On This Long Journey.* New York: Scholastic Paperbacks, 2014.

Conley, Robert J. *The Cherokee.* New York: Chelsea House Publishers, 2011.

Dwyer, Helen, and D.L. Birchfield. *Cherokee History and Culture.* New York: Gareth Stevens Publishing, 2011.

Jones, Veda Boyd. *Nellie the Brave: The Cherokee Trail of Tears.* Uhrichsville, OH: Barbour Books, 2013.

### Works Consulted

*The Cherokee Indian Nation: A Troubled History,* edited by Daniel H. King. Knoxville, TN: The University of Tennessee Press, 1979.

Collier, Peter. *When Shall They Rest? The Cherokees' Long Struggle with America.* New York: Holt, Rinehart, and Winston, 1973.

Ehle, John. *Trail of Tears: The Rise and Fall of the Cherokee Nation.* New York: Anchor Books, 1988.

Mooney, James. *Myths of the Cherokee.* New York: Dover Publications, Inc., 1995.

Perdue, Theda, and Michael D. Green. *The Cherokee Nation and the Trail of Tears.* New York, The Penguin Group, 2007.

Smith, Daniel Blake. *An American Betrayal: Cherokee Patriots and the Trail of Tears.* New York: Henry Holt and Company, 2011.

Treuer, Anton. *Atlas of Indian Nations.* Washington, DC: National Geographic Society, 2013.

Waldman, Carl. *Encyclopedia of Native American Tribes.* New York: Facts on File Publications, 1988.

## On the Internet

Cherokee Environment

http://www.historyforkids.org/learn/northamerica/before1500/environment/cherokee.htm

Cherokee Facts for Kids

http://www.bigorrin.org/cherokee_kids.htm

Cherokee Indians

http://www.indians.org/articles/cherokee-indians.html

Cherokee Nation

http://www.cherokee.org/

Native Arts

http://www.aaanativearts.com/index.htm

Native Languages of the Americas: Cherokee

http://www.native-languages.org/cherokee.htm

**PHOTO CREDITS:** p. 7—Lmaotru; p. 18—Wolfgang Sauber; p. 31—Nfutvol. Cover and all other photos—Public Domain. Every measure has been taken to find all copyright holders of material used in this book. In the event any mistakes or omissions have happened within, attempts to correct them will be made in future editions of the book.

**ancestor** (AN-sess-ter)—A person from whom one is descended.

**conquistador** (kon-KEE-stuh-door)—A Spanish conqueror.

**contaminate** (kun-TAM-ih-nayt)—To make something dirty or impure by adding something harmful.

**deficient** (dih-FISH-int)—Lacking something.

**deteriorate** (dee-TEER-ee-or-ayt)—To fall apart.

**epidemic** (ep-ih-DEH-mik)—A widespread occurrence of an infectious disease.

**fertile** (FUR-tul)—Of land, able to produce healthy crops.

**foliage** (FOH-lij)—The leaves of a plant.

**illuminate** (ih-LOO-muh-nayt)—To brighten with light.

**multitude** (MALL-tih-tood)—A large number of people gathered together.

**null**—Amounting to nothing.

**preside** (prih-ZYD)—To take or be in charge.

**prestigious** (prih-STIH-jis)—Respected, admired.

**regulate** (REG-yuh-layt)—To control or direct by a rule or method.

**Shaman** (SHAH-mun)—A person who acts as a connection between the natural world and the spirit world.

**spontaneous** (spon-TAY-nee-us)—Done or produced without outside help; happening by itself.

# MEET THE
# AUTHOR

**Rusty**

Russell Roberts has researched, written, and published numerous books for both children and adults. Among his books for adults are *Down the Jersey Shore, Historical Photos of New Jersey,* and *Ten Days to a Sharper Memory.* He has written over 50 nonfiction books for children. Roberts often speaks on the subjects of his books before various groups and organizations. He lives in New Jersey.